ROOTS OF SUCCESS

A GRANDMOTHER'S LEGACY

RETINELLA GAYLE

Follow Retinella Gayle

Social Media Outlets:

Facebook: Retinella Gayle

Email: rootsofsuccessbook@gmail.com

CONTENTS

Dedication

This book is dedicated to my grandmother and the strong, resilient women of the world—the countless women who stand as pillars of strength, courage, and resilience. In every corner of the globe; you have faced challenges with grace, reached goals no one thought you could reach, and lit the paths for generations to come. Your stories, sacrifices, and successes are the heartbeat of this dedication.

To my two precious boys, Marlon and Darron Williams: you are the lights of my life and the driving force behind everything I do. Your love, laughter, and unwavering support have been my greatest blessings. May this book be a testament to the endless inspiration you provide.

To my beloved grandchildren: in your innocence, I find hope for a future that you will shape. May the words within these pages reflect the love and wisdom I wish to impart to each of you. As you navigate the journey of life, may you find strength in your roots and courage in your dreams.

Acknowledgement

A heartfelt tribute goes to Profit Churlu Church, my grandmother's church, where my roots in faith were firmly planted from my childhood to adolescence. Mount Assembly Zion Church holds cherished memories of bus trips, parish visits, singing, dancing, and the camaraderie that made it the best time of my life with my beloved grandmother.

I extend my deepest gratitude to the Bronx Miracle Gospel Tabernacle and Word of Faith Ministries for being the spiritual foundation of my journey. Rev. Keith Elijah Thompson and his wife, Yvonne Mae Thompson, deserve special recognition for their guidance and support. My time as an usher and a member of the choir enriched my spirit, and I am thankful for the blessings shared within those sacred walls.

To Rev. Marcia Pennicott, your teachings at Elim Church of God in Mount Vernon have been a source of inspiration and enlightenment. Being a part of this ministry has brought immense joy and growth to my spiritual journey.

My sincere thanks go to Eva Williams, whose unwavering support and the opportunity she provided me at Montefiore have been life-changing. I am forever grateful for her influence and the positive impact she has had on my career. A special mention to Ms. Colon, who, under Eva's guidance, played a pivotal role in granting me the job.

I extend my heartfelt gratitude to two exceptional individuals, Jannelle Ambrose and Dr. Denise Nicholson, whose unwavering dedication and tireless efforts have been instrumental in bringing the ideas within this book to life. Their commitment to helping me articulate the thoughts swirling within my mind has been nothing short of extraordinary.

Jannelle, your creative insight and meticulous attention to detail, have transformed vague ideas into coherent thoughts and stories. Your enthusiasm and relentless support throughout this writing journey have made this collaboration a truly enriching experience.

Dr. Denise Nicholson, your expertise and guidance have been invaluable in shaping the depth of this work. Your scholarly contributions and commitment to clarity have elevated my book to a level I could only dream of achieving on my own.

Together, Jannelle and Dr. Nicholson, you have formed an indispensable team that breathed life into my ideas, turning them into a cohesive and meaningful narrative.

This book stands as a testament that working together creates a spirit that fuels creativity; my book exists today because of the collaborative efforts of these two remarkable individuals and many others; including the team of Bold Publishing. Thank you for your passion, dedication, and the countless hours invested in helping me bring this project to life.

Foreword

Welcome to the poignant and compelling narrative of *Roots of Success: A Grandmother's Legacy*, where the indomitable spirit of Retinella Gayle, affectionately known as Lisa or Sister Lisa, as her church brethren call her, unfolds against the vibrant tapestry of Jamaica's landscapes and the hidden struggles beneath its beauty.

In these pages, Sister Lisa invites you on a captivating journey through the ups and downs of her life, from the challenges of her parents' hardships to the transformative influence of her grandmother in Westmoreland. Her story reflects the resilience that flourished amidst adversity; a testament to the strength embedded in the roots of her Jamaican heritage.

As Lisa's life takes unexpected turns, you will witness the unwavering dedication to family survival that defines her journey. The narrative weaves through the vibrant markets, the hardships of limited education, and the transformative impact of government assistance.

Lisa's determination, especially in the face of abuse, showcases the strength found in seeking refuge and the resilience that arises from facing life's obstacles head-on. The political turmoil of the 1970s becomes an unexpected hurdle, leading to difficult choices that interrupted Lisa's educational pursuits.

In *Roots of Success,* you will be transported into the complexities of Jamaican life, where each triumph and challenge contributes to the legacy of a woman who strives for a better future. Lisa's story resonates as a testament to the unwavering spirit of Jamaican resilience, encapsulating the essence of a woman who, against all odds, emerges victorious in her pursuit of success.

Prepare to be inspired, moved, and enlightened as you turn the pages of *Roots of Success: A Grandmother's Legacy*, a story that transcends borders and speaks to the universal themes of strength, determination, and the enduring power of familial love.

By Dr. Denise Nicholson

Introduction

Embark on a captivating journey through the pages of *Roots of Success: A Grandmother's Legacy* as I, Retinella Gayle, also known as Lisa, or Sister Lisa, share my inspiring life story. I was born in the beautiful land of Jamaica on March 28, 1959, and my story unfolds against the backdrop of the island's beauty and the hidden struggles faced by its people.

The early years of my life in Westmoreland were marked by my parents' hardships, especially my father's battle with alcoholism. At the age of 12, my mother's departure to Kingston left me in the care of my grandmother; immersing me in a world of marketplaces, hard work, and limited education.

Set against the vibrant backdrop of Westmoreland, my story portrays the resilience of my grandmother and the transformative power of support. My dedication to my family's survival became the driving force behind my sacrifices and the invaluable life lessons I learned in the face of adversity.

At 17, I moved to Kingston in pursuit of better opportunities and faced many challenges; including an abusive stepfather and educational obstacles. My determination led me to find refuge with a teacher, showcasing the strength that comes from seeking help in times of need.

Unexpectedly, political turmoil disrupted my education during the 1970s, forcing me to make difficult choices amid the feud between the Jamaica Labour Party (JLP) and the People's National Party (PNP). Threatened due to perceived political affiliation, my educational journey was brought to an abrupt halt.

Roots of Success: A Grandmother's Legacy invites readers to witness the complexities of life in Jamaica and the indomitable strength that carried me through adversity. My story is a testament to the unwavering spirit of a Jamaican woman striving for a better future amidst challenges and triumphs.

Bio

Retinella Gayle, also known as Lisa, is a hard-working, strong, and industrious woman. She understands the value of everything she creates, putting in dedicated hours even into the night. Like a skilled weaver, she spins her own thread and crafts her own cloth, showcasing her creativity and independence.

Lisa's generosity extends to the poor and needy, exemplifying a heart that cares for others. Her kindness is like a warm blanket, offering comfort to those who worry. Even when faced with challenges, she faces them with resilience and doesn't falter, providing her family with the warmth of love and fine clothing.

Lisa creates bedspreads and stylish clothes, showcasing her talent and dedication. In the tapestry of her life, she wears fine, stylish clothing, symbolizing both elegance and strength.

The acronym G.A.Y.L.E, which spells her last name, holds a special meaning for Lisa:

- G: Gorgeous
- A: Awesome & Anger (perhaps representing the strength to overcome challenges)
- Y: Youth (You are as young as you feel)
- L: Love
- E: Excellent & Exotic

Proud of herself, Lisa stands tall in her accomplishments. Her journey is a testament to hard work, creativity, and a generous spirit. In her world, she weaves a story of strength, love, and excellence; leaving an indelible mark on the fabric of life.

Preface

Jamaica, Jamaica, the land of Rasta, Blue Mountain coffee, and tranquil rivers, is one of the best places on Earth. It is also known for the beautiful smiles of the Jamaican people and is the place of my birth. I, Retinella Gayle (no middle name) made my debut during the Easter celebration at midnight on March 28, 1959, amongst bun and cheese and fried fish.

Sometimes, those beautiful Jamaican smiles hide struggle and hardship. I, for one, have walked those roads from humble beginnings, without shoes sometimes. Today, I am achieving the American dream—attaining a comfortable life for myself; with plenty of shoes, I might add.

As I embrace this new chapter of my life—retirement; I look back on the roads that led me here. Even though the path was rocky and challenging at times, I walked with the knowledge that God was forever walking beside me and guiding my every step. My continued faith, love, and praises to Him have blessed me to celebrate yet another birthday—my 65th.

Early Years With My Grandmother

I spent the first 12 years of my life living with my parents, Linda Hill, who was of Maroon descent, and Neiman "Sonny Boy" Gayle, who was of Indian descent. I don't recall much about those years other than my parents' struggles due to my father's alcoholism, which he developed while working at one of the rum factories. His addiction put a tremendous strain on the family. When I was 12, my mother decided she couldn't stand it anymore. She left my father and moved three hours away; to Kingston. Since she needed to settle herself first, she left me, along with my two older sisters, Cynthia and Chiquita, as well as my brother, Carlos, with my grandmother,

Ms. Claribel Rose Whitelock, who lived in Westmoreland.

Westmoreland is the most western parish of Jamaica. Its capital, Savanna-la-Mar, was made into a port for sugar export around 1730. The Spanish name Savanna-la-mar, means, *plain by the sea*—fitting for its location. The areas various rivers and streams sustained the lush vegetation of the area, some of which my grandmother harvested or purchased to support our family. She sold fruits and vegetables at multiple marketplaces, such as Savanna-la-mar, Darliston, Montego Bay, and Kingston. I never knew the reason (maybe because I was the youngest), but my grandmother selected me to accompany her to the market to assist with the selling. I knew this was vital for our family, so I never questioned it, even though it meant that I had to miss school.

My limited education was attained at Coke's View Primary School at age six and later at Petersfield High School. Needless to say, my attendance was inconsistent. Sometimes I could only attend school two days per week; on the other days and Saturdays, I was at the market selling. When I was 14, my grandmother enrolled my sisters and me in a government program that provided money for our care, education, and food. The government funding was a tremendous help, as my parents could not provide financial assistance to support us. My grandmother was doing it all with the income she generated from the market and the money my grandfather occasionally sent home from England.

With the government funding, we improved our living conditions by refurbishing our two-room house and adding a third room. Before the renovation, my grandmother, my two sisters, and I shared a bedroom with two beds while my brother slept in the living room. The renovation allowed us to modify our sleeping arrangements to two per room while my brother remained in the living room.

What I recall most about those formative years was that I was always working. If I wasn't at the market selling, then I would be in the kitchen cooking or cleaning. My sisters didn't have to pitch in as much. My brother was tasked with climbing trees to pick fruits such as mangoes, limes, ackee and plums; or traveling to other areas to buy the fruits and vegetables; bringing them to the market for me to sell with my grandmother. When I was a bit older, and my grandmother couldn't go to the market as much due to her arthritis, my brother would assist me with carrying the goods to the bus. My sisters never had to go to the markets to sell.

My one bright light was worshiping under the trees in the Zion churchyard. On Sunday mornings, I would wake at 6 or 7 o'clock to cook, bathe in the river, oil up my skin, comb my hair, put on my Sunday best and walk to church barefoot; my grandmother couldn't afford to buy us church shoes. I loved participating in all the church activities—from their Christmas programs to the choir and field trips to other churches. There would be pure excitement in the church when the congregation loved one of our recitals and members would do a 'money pull-up'. It gave us kids a sense of joy and pride. I became good at memorizing verses and prayers; this aided me whenever I was called upon. It also concealed my struggle with reading. Praise and worship are my favorite parts of church to this day; I enjoy singing and dancing while praising the Almighty.

When it came to church and church activities, my grandmother had no objections; but outside of the church, there was nothing but work—no going to the beach, no playing with other kids, and no just running around as a kid. Whenever my dad visited us occasionally from Grange Hill, where he resided with his mother, we would go down by the river to talk. My mother never came back to Westmoreland to visit. The only time I saw her was when she would stop by the market in Kingston when my grandmother and I were there selling.

Looking back now, I realize that I was the heartbeat of my family—the vital organ that kept going for our survival—sacrificing everything. Missing school, and doing all the hard work, was the key to that survival. Those years taught me life lessons that I would have never learned from a book. The lessons I learned included how to stretch a dollar and manage limited resources. I also learned that you have to work for any and everything you want in life as nothing will be handed to you.

My young life was characterized by hard work, limited education and the unwavering support of my grandmother. I recognize the resilience that shaped my journey. The daily sacrifice my grandmother instilled in me; good work ethic, adaptability and perseverance.

The sacrifices made for survival, the lessons learned in the marketplaces of Westmoreland and the transformations brought by government assistance are threads woven into the fabric of my life. This chapter of my life laid the foundation for the continued challenges to come and the pursuit of a brighter future.

Dreaming of an Education

By the time I turned 17, all the hard work had taken a toll on me. One day when my mother came to the market to visit, I nervously approached her and asked if I could live with her in Kingston. I thought Kingston would have more opportunities for me than Westmoreland did. To my surprise, my mother agreed to me moving in with her and her family at their two-room dwelling in a Kingston tenement yard. By that time, my mother had remarried and had three more children—my sisters, Angela and Nadean, and brother, Bobby. I also had a new stepsister, Dawnette, who was around my age.

Life didn't instantly become easier with this move. I had to find work to continue supporting myself and help my mother carry her cooked food to the market, where she sold it to earn her living. I didn't have to assist her with the selling, however.

As the adage says, *God helps those who help themselves*. I always wanted to go back to school and one day I stopped thinking about it and just did it. I enrolled in the Tivoli Garden High School to continue my education. I was able to do this as I was still in the government program. It wasn't easy living with my mother as my stepfather was abusive. This led me to move in with a cousin, but her husband also tried to abuse me. Providentially, I was able to find refuge with one of my teachers. *God is our refuge and strength, a very present help in trouble. Psalms 46:1.*

I was just trying to get my education to better my life, but something always kept getting in my way. At that time, there was a long-standing feud between the two main political parties in

Jmaiaca—the Jamaica Labour Party (JLP) and the People's National Party (PNP). In 1976, more than a hundred people were murdered during the turmoil, as political parties formed paramilitary divisions, and by 1978, Jamaican soldiers had massacred five JLP supporters. Immediately, my dreams of getting an education started to crumble.

I tried my best to stay under the radar during that time and took safety measures such as removing the tie and crest that were a part of my school uniform when I rode the bus. I only wore them in the schoolyard. However, one day while on the bus, a girl targeted me and threatened my life; claiming that I was from the PNP area. I ain't no fighter, so I had no choice but to drop out of school to avoid this threat. I feared that she would attack me on my way to the bus stop.

Becoming a Mother

At the age of 19, my life took a dramatic turn; I became a mom. Even though I was no longer living with my mother, I traveled back and forth to visit her, and I did the same with my grandmother. While visiting my mom, I met my first love; a slightly older young jockey named Lisset Williams, who lived in the tenement yard with his family. He always made conversation with me, bought me things and accompanied me to the bus. When my teacher realized I was pregnant, I had to move out; Dawnette, my stepsister, and I decided to move into a one-bedroom house together.

My bouncing baby boy, Marlon Williams, was born on February 6, 1978. I continued to live with Dawnette during the first year of his life;

by the time Marlon turned two, my boyfriend, and now my child's father Lisset, was able to get us one of those affordable project homes, so we moved in together. I had my own little family.

On July 8, 1981, I welcomed my second bouncing baby boy, Derron Williams. To help support my family, I worked as a sales associate in a wholesale store, made brassieres at the Freezone factory and started my own little business. I bought clothes and leather from Haiti, Panama, and Venezuela and resold them. I saved money from each paycheck to purchase US dollars, which I used to travel down to South America to source the items. It was challenging, as sometimes I had difficulty getting the things released from customs and had to save money again to pay for the clearance. But I didn't let it deter me. I always did what I had to do to make ends meet.

Bound for a New Horizon: From Jamaica to Canada, A Rocky Start in the Great North

Although I was doing well, I still longed for higher education and I enrolled myself in different continuing educational programs, such as hairdressing, home economics, technical training and early childcare. Sometimes I had to stop as I could not afford the tuition, or there were scheduling conflicts; plus I had to be there for my two boys. Despite all the stumbling blocks, I always remembered how hard my grandmother worked and the lessons she taught me to never give up and to make something of myself. That's what kept me going and pushed me to better myself.

After a couple of years of this routine and the good tidings I had been hearing about the great Canada and America, I decided to apply for a Canadian visa to seek new opportunities. It was a hard decision to make as I knew it meant leaving the boys in the care of their father and his mother, but I knew that it was for the best and that, in the long run, it would be beneficial for them.

In 1989, at the age of 30, I migrated to Canada upon being approved for my visa. My arrival in Canada started out rocky. After I purchased my ticket and notified my cousin of my arrival time and date, she told me she couldn't pick me up from the airport. This caused me to panic as I was about to go to another country—an unfamiliar place and I had no idea how to get around. Luckily, I had a girlfriend, Jackie, in Canada who was able to pick me up from the airport and she let me stay with her for a little while.

Eventually, I met up with my cousin, who had a home care agency, and I was able to secure employment right away. God was always there making a way for me. I recall one of my favorite scriptures: Psalms 91: V 1-6

1)*Whoever dwells in the shelter of the Most High will rest in the shadow of the Almighty. 2) I will say of the Lord, 'He is my refuge and my fortress, my God, in whom I trust.' 3) Surely he will save you from the fowler's snare and from the deadly pestilence. 4) He will cover you with his feathers, and under his wings you will find refuge; his faithfulness will be your shield and rampart. 5) You will not fear the terror of night, nor the arrow that flies by day, 6) nor the pestilence that stalks in the darkness, nor the plague that destroys at midday.*

I was doing a live-in home care job. Plus, I also worked as a night cleaner for a restaurant. I was always running from one job to the next, saving most of my money as I didn't have to pay rent at the apartment. I was also able to send home funds to assist my family. I even managed to open a bank account in Canada even though I didn't have adequate paperwork, as my cousin had a contact in a bank.

I decided that I wanted to stay in North America. My Canadian visa was for one year, after which I needed to leave the country. I didn't want to return to Jamaica, so I applied for a US visa and my cousin had someone lined up to file for me. The plan was for me to go to the US to complete the interview part of the application and then return to Canada, but as the saying goes: *Man plans and God laughs.*

Everything was set. I would go to the US for my immigration interview at Federal Plaza in New York and then return to Canada. I made arrangements with my uncle to pick me up from the airport. However, I was surprised to discover that there was a New York airport and a Newark airport in New Jersey. I learned this the hard way when my flight arrived at Newark Airport, and no one was there to pick me up.

I waited patiently, thinking that my uncle was running late, but hours passed. This was the early 1990s, so there were no cell phones, and my calls to their home phone went unanswered for hours. Eventually, I was able to contact my friend Jennifer who agreed to let me stay with her. I spent over eight hours at Newark airport before taking a cab at 3 am to Jennifer's house. Jennifer lived on Rosewood Avenue, off White Plains Road, in the Bronx. When I finally connected with my uncle, I was told he went to LaGuardia airport to pick me up; that's how I found out about the different airports in the region. As one door closed, another one opened; God's favor was always with me.

My cab driver was from Albania— he barely spoke English, and didn't know his way around the Bronx. To this day, I remember the drive. We drove up the Bronx River Parkway and saw how wooded and dark the area was. I said, "The area looks like the countryside of Jamaica." I thought, *America is supposed to be more well-kept and developed. Oh, I have come to a foreign country to stay in the bush.* The driver had a hard time finding the address. Of course, this was long before GPS but with God's help, I got to Jennifer's safely— at about 5 am.

I thank God for the grace of Jennifer and her family. I have no idea what would have happened to me without them. On the day of my interview, Jennifer's sister, Amerie, accompanied me to Manhattan to the Federal Plaza building. The interview went well, but I was told I needed to return to Canada to await their decision. The only problem was that I didn't know how to get back to Newark airport, and there wasn't anyone there to take me; everyone had gone to work. I was then stuck in New York, crashing on Jennifer's couch.

I didn't let getting stuck keep me from losing my Jamaican smile, however. No way! At the time, Jennifer's mom was a live-in home care attendant, and she made arrangements for me to take her weekend shifts. I would travel to the home in Queens on Fridays to relieve her, and she would return on Monday mornings to relieve me. When everyone left the house, I walked the streets looking for work and was able to find an off-the-books job cleaning at a furniture store. These two little gigs helped sustain me and allowed me to contribute to the household. I did these jobs for a few months until a friend I had made in the apartment building introduced me to a home care agency on White Plains Road, where I was able to get another part-time home-care job. My cousin was able to use her contact in the bank to close my Canadian bank account and send the funds to me. The closure of the account signified the conclusion of my Canadian chapter.

Proverbs 31:30

"Charm is deceptive, and beauty is fleeting; but a woman who fears the Lord is to be praised."

"I do not wish women to have power
over men; but over themselves."

— **Mary Shelley**

Proverbs 3:5

"Trust in the LORD with all your heart
and lean not on your own understanding."

"There are two powers in the world; one is the sword and the other is the pen. There is a third power stronger than both, that of women."

— **Malala Yousafzai**

Exodus 15:2

"The Lord is my strength and my song,
and he has become my salvation; this is my
God, and I will praise him, my father's
God, and I will exalt him."

"Good friends, good books, and a sleepy
conscience: this is the ideal life."

— **Mark Twain**

Proverbs 1:8

"Hear, my son, your father's instruction,
and forsake not your mother's teaching."

Acts 10:2

"He and all his family were devout and God-fearing; he gave generously to those in need and prayed to God regularly."

Deuteronomy 31:6

"Be strong and courageous. Do not fear or
be in dread of them, for it is the Lord
your God who goes with you. He will
not leave you or forsake you."

"True friends are never apart, maybe in distance but never in heart."

— **Unknown**

Psalm 73:26

"My flesh and my heart may fail, but
God is the strength of my heart
and my portion forever."

"Never leave a friend behind. Friends are all we have to get us through this life-and they are the only things from this world that we could hope to see in the next."

— **Dean Koontz**

"Call it a clan, call it a network, call it a tribe, call it a family: Whatever you call it, whoever you are, you need one."

— Jane Howard

Proverbs 30:5

"Every word of God is flawless; He is a shield to those who take refuge in Him."

"She is more than a good woman
and a good person. She is a beautiful
soul who carries light in her smile
and love in her bones."

— Bhoomika Cs

Proverbs 3:5

"Trust in the LORD with all your heart
and lean not on your own understanding."

"A good woman is one who loves passionately, has guts, seriousness and passionate convictions, takes responsibility, and shapes society."

– Betty Friedan

Psalm 18:2

"The Lord is my rock, and my fortress,
and my deliverer; my God, my strength,
in whom I will trust."

"Once I learned to like me more than others, then I didn't have to worry about being the funniest, most popular, or prettiest. I was the best me and I only ever tried to be that."

— Issa Rae

"The world needs strong women. Women who will lift and build others, who will love and be loved, women who live bravely, both tender and fierce, women of indomitable will."

— **Amy Tenney**

"She was powerful not because she wasn't scared but because she went on so strongly, despite the fear."

— Atticus

Psalm 91:1

"He who dwells in the shelter of the Most High will abide in the shadow of the Almighty."

Proverbs 17:22

"A cheerful heart is good medicine, but a
crushed spirit dries up the bones."

Philippians 4:19

"And my God will meet all your
needs according to the riches of his
glory in Christ Jesus."

"Be a first-rate version of yourself, not a second-rate version of someone else."

— Judy Garland

African Queen

"Real power is born of the humility and grace of sisterhood. That's what empowerment means. The more power you share, the more power you have, and the more power you have, the more you must share."

— Kerry Washington

Love and light I give to you

The best is yet to come

"No matter what happens, or how bad it seems today, life does go on, and it will be better tomorrow."

— Maya Angelou

Psalm 20:1

"May the LORD answer you when you
are in distress; may the name of the
God of Jacob protect you."

"You have to have confidence in your ability,
and then be tough enough to follow through."

— Rosalynn Carter

Psalms 20:6

"Now this I know: The LORD gives victory to his anointed. He answers him from his heavenly sanctuary with the victorious power of his right hand."

Isaiah 40:29

"He gives strength to the weary and
increases the power of the weak."

Psalms 20: 7

"Some trust in chariots and some in
horses, but we trust in the name
of the LORD our God."

Reaching for the American Dream

My American chapter started with me constantly on the run, hustling hard. The home-care agency initially had me working two days a week for $5 an hour. On the weekends, I still held on to the home-care job in Queens. The home-care agency then found me a new placement, working night shifts at a home in Riverdale. So, I worked the furniture cleaning job during the day and then rushed to my night job in Riverdale. I hustled hard for a couple of years, always with two or three jobs to ensure that I could make ends meet and send money back home to take care of the kids. Throughout the running around, I never forgot to thank God for always walking beside me; I attended church regularly.

After one year, I saved enough money to move into a $ 600-a-month, one-bedroom, garage apartment. I eventually left the furniture cleaning job to work as a sales associate in a boutique in Mount Vernon. I enjoyed working there as I love fashion and dressing up. I kept my Riverdale job, though. I was always on the go, catching three buses to travel between home and the two jobs daily. I remember having to stand outside in the bitter cold in the winter—freezing while waiting for the bus. That was no fun. That was what made me decide that I needed to get a driver's license.

Time kept moving forward, but I didn't pay it any mind as I was too busy to stop and notice. Along the way, Lisset, my children's father, received his US visa and joined me in New York. I connected him with the people at the furniture store where I used to work, to get him a job, but with the time that had passed, we had grown apart and decided to go our separate ways. The boys at that time were pre-teens and were living with their paternal grandmother and an aunt who assisted with their care. Marlon was on a swim team that traveled occasionally for swim meets, and it so happened that the team was scheduled to travel to Florida. I saw this as an excellent opportunity to get the boys.

I sent the money home to get Derron's passport and US visa so he could travel with Marlon. Lisset then traveled down to Florida to collect the boys and bring them to New York. I was finally reunited with my boys after so many years. My one-bedroom was a tight fit for the three of us, but we made it work.

The boys slept on a pullout couch, and I cooked so they had food when they came home from school. Before heading to the Riverdale job, I always came home to check on the boys, and their father and a neighbor also looked out for them.

Was it the best? No. Was it easy? No, we were struggling; but it was what we had to do to get by in this country, and we were thankful for what we had every day. Just like how my grandmother had made her small home, work for me and my siblings, I knew that this home would have to work for us. I learned from my grandmother that all things work for good, to those who love the Lord, as the scripture says.

Prayer was my pathway for daily strength, and still is today. After a few years, the boys decided that they wanted to live with their dad, who had an apartment with more space.

Finally Getting My Education: Becoming a Nursing Assistant

In 1993 I completed my nurse's aide/ nursing assistant training at ABC Training Center. This was my second attempt to complete the course. The first time didn't work out, as the other training center required a work permit or proof of citizenship, so I had to discontinue that program. With my new certification, I was hired by an agency called Staff Builders, and I was placed in a Senior Quarters Assisted Living Residence, in Stamford, Connecticut.

Due to the long commute, I had to give up my job at the boutique. I didn't dwell on that as I had managed to pick up a night job taking care of an elderly lady in Greenwich. I worked at the Senior Quarters for about five years where I received Employee of the Month a few times and earned several different certifications.

I truly enjoyed my time at the Senior Quarters. I worked with the dementia residents and would have a blast singing and dancing with them. We took field trips to the beach, had scenic bus rides, and enjoyed sweet treats like ice cream. After a few years, the dementia department closed, and I was offered the position of dining hall supervisor—my most significant accomplishment. I oversaw the hiring of people and setting up of the dining hall. The only dark cloud was the chef, who constantly argued if the residents decided to change their meal choices. I was like, "Come on man, they are old so you need to have patience with them." But I didn't let him rain on our parade.

In April 1999, I started working at Stamford Hospital. Initially, I was doing one-to-one jobs before working as a housekeeper. Meanwhile, I was attending the J. M Wright Regional

Vocational Technical School to get my Certified Nursing Assistant (CNA) certification. Once, while emptying a patient's garbage, I recall the patient asking me why a pretty girl like me was taking out the trash, and I responded that somebody had to do it; but I was working hard to get my CNA license. Around the same time, I got my driver's license. I rented a car from Enterprise every weekend and drove to work in Connecticut to get accustomed to the highway. When the employee from Enterprise collected the car, I always told him to bring it back the next weekend.

I wasn't successful with my first attempt at the CNA test; for the second time around, I pushed myself harder. I would study while driving to Connecticut by listening to the lectures and asking the nurses in the hospital to help me study. I was nervous about taking the test again and hoped and prayed that I would pass as I couldn't handle the embarrassment of the nurses knowing that I took the test twice and failed both times. I always remembered the scripture, Philippians 4, 6-7: *Do not be anxious about anything, but in every situation, by prayer and petition, with thanksgiving, present your requests to God. And the peace of God, which transcends all understanding, will guard your hearts and your minds in Christ Jesus.*

On June 15, 2000, I received my CNA license. I did it! I passed my exams! I transitioned from housekeeping to being a nursing assistant at Stamford Hospital; I worked there for eight years. Part of my duties was to do finger sticks, draw blood, and do EKGs. It was during my tenure at Stamford Hospital that a friend of mine, Ms. Doris, who was a realtor, told me about a small two-bedroom house with a basement that was being sold on Allerton Avenue, in the Bronx. I had been renting at the two other locations where I lived, so I jumped at the opportunity to purchase my own home.

The house was a foreclosure for around $120,000. I presented my tax papers and down payment and purchased that home, even though I still wasn't a permanent resident.

Becoming a Homeowner

My son Marlon and I moved into our new home and I rented the basement to a hairdresser. Derron was still living with his father, who lived in Maryland at that time.

I met my second love, Mr. Kenny Robinson, while working at the Senior Quarter and we stayed in contact after I changed jobs. He worked in maintenance at the nursing home and always assisted me when delivering the patient's food. We connected and decided to marry at the New Rochelle courthouse. It was an intimate affair with only one of my neighbors and Marlon as our witnesses. Mr. Kenny moved into the new house on Allerton Avenue with Marlon and me.

Things were going well; I loved Mr. Kenny. He was a nice guy, but he had some demons that I only became aware of after the wedding. When he was 17, he joined the army, and by the time he left, he was battling post-traumatic stress disorder (PTSD). He turned to alcohol and drugs to numb his pain. We tried to make it work. He even went to rehab in Pennsylvania, where I would often visit him. When he returned from rehab, we would have a few good months before it got bad again. He drained our checking account, not leaving any money for the mortgage payment. He even crashed my car, which I had saved up to purchase. After a while, I had to ask him to leave. Mr. Kenny eventually filed for divorce.

A few years later, I met Ms. Jackie, who knew my father. She encouraged me to look for a job at Montefiore Hospital as they offered a better salary. She passed my resume to her sister who was a manager at Montefiore, and I was called in for an interview. I got the job at Montefiore Hospital where I worked part-time. I left Stamford and worked at Montefiore three days a week; I worked the other days at Morningside Nursing Home.

Becoming a Grandmother

One of the happiest moments of my life was when I became a grandma for the first time on May 17, 2004, to Saniya Hyacinth Williams. I absolutely love spending time with her and watching her grow over the years. I remember when she was younger and would come to visit me; we baked banana cake and had fun. It is so hard to believe that she is now an independent adult in college.

As the years passed I continued to hustle; always working two jobs. Eventually, I started working at Montefiore full-time while doing private home care in Connecticut through an agency. I worked the 3 pm - 11 pm shift at Montefiore, then went home, slept for four or five hours, got up and hit the road to drive to Connecticut. Amidst everything, I never forgot to put God first and continue to do my morning praise and worship.

One of my favorite songs to play in the morning is " Where would I be without you?" I also love the song below:

I Speak Jesus

by Charity Gayle

Lyrics

I just wanna speak the name of Jesus

Over every heart and every mind

'Cause I know there is peace within Your presence

I speak Jesus

I just wanna speak the name of Jesus

'Til every dark addiction starts to break

Declaring there is hope and there is freedom

I speak Jesus

'Cause Your name is power

Your name is healing

Your name is life

Break every stronghold

Shine through the shadows

Burn like a fire

I just wanna speak the name of Jesus

Over fear and all anxiety

To every soul held captive by depression

I speak Jesus

'Cause Your name is power

Your name is healing

Your name is life

Break every stronghold

Shine through the shadows

Burn like the fire

Shout Jesus from the mountains

Jesus in the streets

Jesus in the darkness over every enemy

Jesus for my family

I speak the holy name

Jesus, oh

Shout Jesus from the mountains

Jesus in the streets

Jesus in the darkness over every enemy

Jesus for my family

I speak the holy name

Jesus (Jesus)

'Cause Your name is power

Your name is healing

Your name is life

Break every stronghold

Shine through the shadows

Burn like a fire

Your name is power (Your name is power)

Your name is healing (Your name is healing)

Your name is life (You are my life)

Break every stronghold (break every stronghold)

Shine through the shadows

Burn like a fire

I just wanna speak the name of Jesus

Over every heart and every mind

'Cause I know there is peace within Your presence

I speak Jesus

Now A Citizen of
The United States

On April 13, 2007, I became a naturalized American citizen. I had attained the American dream.

In October 2008, I purchased a multi-family townhouse on 221st Street in the Bronx. The house on Allerton needed severe repairs to the sewage system. Whenever I thought the issue was fixed, the yard would back up with water; I didn't want to deal with it anymore.

In spite of all the busyness of my life, I remained an active member of the Bronx Miracle church for years. I attended different functions and met many new friends. However, I currently attend the Elim Church of God, in Mount Vernon. As the saying goes, *all work and no play makes Jane a dull girl;* I have always had an active social life. I love traveling, attending parties, and meeting up with friends for brunch, boat rides or any events. In the past, I played tennis and modeled in Manhattan. I also became a grandma for the second time when Marlon welcomed his son, Jayden Marlon Williams, on July 19, 2010.

Whenever I am in Florida, where Marlon and his family live, I have to cook up some curried goat and rice and peas for my grandson; it's his favorite dish.

The time I spend with my grandchildren reminds me of the days with my grandmother. I learned to listen to them as my grandmother listened to me.

On September 18, 2010, I married Mr. Donald Moore from Jamaica. He is the brother of one of my friends from church. We started out with a long-distance relationship that blossomed, but it wasn't meant to be. We divorced after about nine years of marriage. I am ok for now with my single life. I have enough family and friends around, and who knows, I might meet Mr. Right in my golden years.

On March 17, 2015, Derron welcomed his first and only child, Derron Jr., whom I affectionately call, Mr. Derron. He is a pure joy to be around. I remember taking him to the park when he was younger and whenever he was with me, he wanted to go to Target to buy pizza bagels. I love spending time with my three grandchildren.

With Marlon down in Florida, I saw it as an opportunity to purchase a retirement home down there. Now, I am looking forward to relaxing in Florida at my ranch-style home during my retirement days. I still plan to keep myself active by working part-time with the private home care agency and traveling back and forth between Florida and the Bronx. I also plan to keep my social calendar packed and do a bit of traveling. I love to travel and have traveled to many different places throughout The United States and around the world. I will share some of the places that I have traveled.

Places I Have Visited

Canada

New York

New Jersey

Virginia

North & South Carolina

Georgia

Tennessee

Alabama

Pennsylvania

Ohio

Delaware

Washington DC.

Florida

Arizona

Las Vegas

Vermont

Lake George, NY

Boston

Massachusetts

Panama

Turks & Caicos

Cozumel, Mexico

Trinidad

London, England

Traveling to all these places means the world to me, adding diverse colors to the canvas of my life. Each destination holds a unique significance, contributing to the rich tapestry of my experiences.

Canada represents the wide landscapes and cultural diversity. It embodies the huge amount of opportunities I've explored. New York and New Jersey embody the hustle and bustle of city life, where I navigated challenges with resilience.

Virginia, North & South Carolina, Georgia and Tennessee symbolize a journey through Southern charm, each state adding a chapter to my story. Alabama and Pennsylvania bring encounters with history and tradition, while Ohio and Delaware add more layers to my exploration.

Washington DC, the nation's capital, resonates with political and cultural significance; deepening my understanding of the world. Florida and Arizona offer a mix of relaxation and vibrant landscapes, portraying the balance in my life.

Las Vegas, Vermont, Lake George, Boston, and Connecticut represent moments of leisure and adventure; providing a break from the routine. Massachusetts, Panama, Turks & Caicos, Cozumel, Mexico, and Trinidad bring an international flavor, showcasing the diversity of cultures I've embraced.

London, England, stands as a symbol of my global exploration, reflecting on the interconnectedness of humanity. Each place I've visited becomes a part of my narrative, contributing to my growth, broadening my perspectives, and adding layers to the vibrant story I share in my book. So many of the wonderful places I had the opportunity to visit and learn about were made possible by the warm embrace of my cousins from the

Rose family. The adventures and journeys across so many different destinations became a reality through our connection during our family reunion. These gatherings not only strengthened our family bonds but also opened doors to exploration and discovery. The shared experiences and collective spirit of our family have made me well-traveled and have allowed me to create cherished memories that are deeply rooted in the love and connection we share.

The Lord bless you and keep you; the Lord make his face shine on you and be gracious to you; the Lord turn his face toward you and give you peace. Numbers 6:24-26

Closing Words

So, we've come to the end of Lisa's amazing story in "Roots of Success: A Grandmother's Legacy" Before we say goodbye, let's talk about something special – her time spent working in hospitals. Picture it; a bustling place where lots of different people work together; doctors, nurses, and others. They all team up to help make sick people feel better.

Now, Lisa has been through a lot in her life, from growing up in Jamaica to chasing her dreams in America. But guess what? Just like the hospital, her story is filled with different jobs and challenges. It's like a big puzzle where everyone plays a part.

In the hospitals where she has worked, we

learned that every job is important. The doctors are like the leaders, but the people cleaning the floors are just as crucial. It's a big team working together to help patients. Teamwork makes everything better!

But here's the thing – sometimes, some people think certain jobs are not as important. Lisa faced that challenge too. Some folks didn't see how amazing she was. But you know what? Lisa found pride in her work, no matter what others thought.

Her journey isn't just about work; it's about her life. From a simple start in Jamaica to working in the hospitals, Lisa talks about how proud she is. And guess what? Her family is proud too! Her story is about being strong, proud and working together to reach goals. Lisa's story is like a dance where every little step counts; resulting in a beautiful tune of healing and hope.

Life had tough parts, but Lisa jumped over every hurdle to succeed. As she heads into retirement, her smile shines bright – a symbol of a happy and successful life. So, even if things get tricky, remember, like Lisa, you can overcome challenges and make your own happy story!

Summary

Roots of Success: A Grandmother's Legacy unfolds the remarkable life story of Retinella Gayle, affectionately known as Lisa, as she traces her steps from the vibrant landscapes of Jamaica to the pursuit of the American dream. Born in 1959, Lisa's early life was painted with the colors of both beauty and struggle, encapsulating the essence of Jamaican resilience and the pursuit of success.

The narrative commences with Lisa's childhood in Westmoreland, Jamaica, marked by the challenges of familial hardships and limited educational opportunities. Despite facing obstacles, Lisa embraced her role as the "heartbeat" of her family, navigating through the adversities with unwavering determination and a deep sense of responsibility.

As the pages turn, readers witness Lisa's transition into adulthood, marked by the birth of her two sons, Marlon and Derron, and her relentless pursuit of a better life. The narrative takes a turn as Lisa sets foot on North American soil, first in Canada and eventually in the United States, facing unexpected challenges and embracing growth opportunities.

The reader is guided through Lisa's experiences as she weaves her way through various jobs, educational pursuits, and personal relationships. From being a housekeeper in Stamford, Connecticut, to obtaining her Certified Nursing Assistant (CNA) license, Lisa's journey is a testament to her resilience and unyielding commitment to self-improvement.

Through marriages, divorces, and the joys of grandmotherhood, Lisa's narrative reflects the tapestry of a life well-lived. Her dedication to family, faith, and hard work is evident as she attains American citizenship, purchases homes, and builds a successful career in the healthcare industry.

Roots of Success: A Grandmother's Legacy is more than just a memoir—it is a celebration of Jamaican culture, the pursuit of dreams, and the triumph of an individual over life's adversities. Lisa's story invites readers to reflect on the importance of perseverance, gratitude, and the indomitable spirit that propels one from humble beginnings to the fulfillment of dreams.

As Lisa embarks on the new chapter of retirement, the reader is left inspired by the enduring smile that has weathered the storms, basked in triumphs, and continues to radiate the warmth of a life well-lived.

RETINELLA GAYLE